STATIONS OF TI

A devotion using

The Revelations of Divine Love

of

JULIAN OF NORWICH

THE STATIONS OF THE CROSS

From the earliest days of the church, pilgrims to Jerusalem have followed the path Jesus trod from the house of Pontius Pilate, where he was condemned, to Calvary's Cross and the Sepulchre. In the Middle Ages those who were unable to travel to the Holy Land began to retrace the journey in their own church, where they often set up pictures of the incidents on that journey to help their devotion. Each picture became a "station" where they would stop to meditate and to pray. Today the Stations of the Cross are generally used in Lent, and on Fridays throughout the year.

In this book, the paintings depicting the Stations of the Cross are those designed by Irene Ogden in 1993 for St Julian's church in Norwich, where the 14th century mystic Julian of Norwich lived as an anchoress and wrote her book *The Revelations of Divine Love*. Sheila Upjohn has chosen readings from Julian's book and from Scripture which help deepen our understanding of Our Lord's Passion. These are followed by a prayer. Each Station begins and ends with the traditional acclamations. It is sometimes the custom to kneel briefly at "We adore you O Christ…"

The Stations can be used individually or by a group. The devotion can also be used as an intercession, remembering various people and causes at each Station.

I. CHRIST IS BROUGHT BEFORE PILATE

My kingdom is not of this world. Everyone that is of the truth hears my voice Jn18: 36, 37

Leader We adore you O Christ and we bless you
All Because by your Holy Cross you have redeemed the world.

Luke 23: 13-24
Pilate then summoned the chief priest and the leading men and the people. "You have brought this man before me," he said "as a political agitator. Now I have gone into the matter myself in your presence and found no case against the man...so I shall have him flogged and then let him go." But as one man they shouted "Away with him! Give us Barabbas!" (This man had been thrown into prison for causing a riot in the city and for murder). Pilate was anxious to set Jesus free and addressed them again, but they shouted back: "Crucify him! Crucify him!" .... Pilate then gave his verdict: their demand was to be granted.

Julian Reading
All that our Lord does is rightful, and all that he allows is praiseworthy. And in these two, both good and evil are included. I do not say that evil is praiseworthy, but that our Lord's allowing it is praiseworthy.... And understanding all this, I thought it was impossible that all manner of thing should be well, as our Lord showed me. And I had no other answer from our Lord except this: "What is impossible for you is not impossible for me. I shall keep my word in all things, and I shall make all things well."

Prayers Lord, who accepted a mockery of human justice without resentment, make us willing to bear injustice and to become prisoners for your sake.
All Hear us and heal us, O Lord.

Leader Let us proclaim the mystery of our redemption
All Lord, by your cross and resurrection you have set us free. You are the saviour of the world.

II. CHRIST TAKES UP HIS CROSS

Surely he has borne our griefs and carried our sorrows

Isa 53: 4

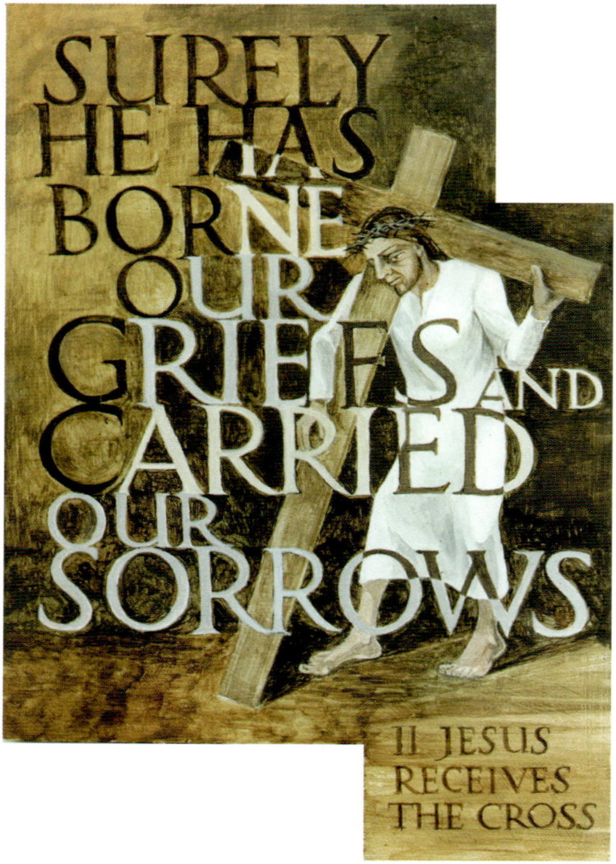

Leader We adore you O Christ and we bless you
All Because by your Holy Cross you have redeemed the world.

John 19: 1-6 & 17
Pilate then had Jesus taken away and scourged; and after this, the soldiers twisted some thorns into a crown and put it on his head, and dressed him in a purple robe... Pilate came outside again and said to them "I am going to bring him out to you to let you see that I find no case". Jesus then came out wearing the crown of thorns and the purple robe. Pilate said "Here is the man"...The chief priest and the guards shouted "Crucify him!" So Pilate handed him over to them to be crucified. They then took charge of Jesus, and carrying his own cross, he went out of the city to the place of the skull, or as it was called in Hebrew, Golgotha.

Julian Reading
I saw the body bleeding freely from the wounds made by the scourging. The fair skin was driven deep into the tender flesh by the harsh striking all over the sweet body.. And then it came into my mind that God has made many waters in earth for our use and our comfort, because of his dear love for us. But yet it pleases him better that we should simply and humbly take his blessed blood to wash away our sins... And after this, before God spoke any word, he allowed me to look on him for a while. Then he formed these words in my soul: "By this is the fiend overcome."

Prayers Lord, who bore the Cross made heavy by our sins, help us to carry the cross you have chosen for us and let us always see your footsteps before us on the road.
All Hear us and heal us, O Lord.

Leader Let us proclaim the mystery of our redemption
All Lord, by your cross and resurrection you have set us free. You are the saviour of the world.

III. CHRIST FALLS

He was despised and rejected. He was wounded for our transgressions Isa 53: 5

Leader We adore you O Christ and we bless you
All Because by your Holy Cross you have redeemed the world

Hebrews 4: 14 & 15
Since in Jesus, the Son of God, we have the supreme priest who has gone through to the highest heaven, we must never let go of the faith we have professed. For it is not as if we had a high priest who is incapable of feeling our weaknesses with us; but we have one who has been tempted in every way that we are, though he is without sin.

Julian reading
And I saw it is his will that we know that he does not take the fall of any one of those who shall be saved any harder than he took the fall of Adam. And we know that he loved Adam endlessly, and looked after him safely in his need - and that now he has blessedly restored him in high unimaginable joys….. And so now we have matter for mourning, because our sin is the cause of Christ's pain. And now we have lasting cause to rejoice, because endless love made him suffer.

Prayers Lord, who fell beneath the weight of the Cross, open our eyes to the pain and injury our sins inflict, so we may come to hate sin as you hate it and love truth as you love it. Bring us repentance. Turn our bitterness to hope.
All Hear us and heal us, O Lord.

Leader Let us proclaim the mystery of our redemption
All Lord, by your cross and resurrection you have set us free. You are the saviour of the world.

IV. CHRIST MEETS HIS MOTHER

I know him and the fellowship of his suffering being made comformable to his death Mk 8: 34

Leader We adore you O Christ and we bless you
All Because by your Holy Cross you have redeemed the world

Luke 2: 34-35
As the child's father and mother stood there, wondering at the things that were being said about him, Simeon blessed them and said to Mary his mother, "You see this child. He is destined for the fall and rising of many in Israel, destined to be a sign that is rejected - and a sword will pierce your own soul too - so that the secrets thoughts of many may be laid bare."

Julian reading
Here I saw part of the compassion of our Lady, Saint Mary, for she and Christ were so joined in love that the greatness of her love caused the greatness of her grief. And so, in this, I saw the instinctive love, led on by grace, that all creation has for him... Our Lord showed me Our Lady, St Mary, to teach us this: that it was the wisdom and truth in her, when she beheld her Maker, that enabled her to know him as so great, so holy - and so mighty, and so good.

Prayers Lord, who grew up in a family and who gave us your Mother to be our mother too, we ask you to become part of our families and of your family the church, and to transform them by your love. Make us truly your children.
All Hear us and heal us, O Lord.

Leader Let us proclaim the mystery of our redemption
All Lord, by your cross and resurrection you have set us free. You are the saviour of the world.

V. SIMON HELPS CHRIST CARRY HIS CROSS

Whoever will come after me let him take up his cross and follow me Mk 8: 34

Leader We adore you O Christ and we bless you
All Because by your Holy Cross you have redeemed the world

Luke 23: 26
As they were leading him away, they seized on a man, Simon from Cyrene, who was coming in from the country, and made him shoulder the cross and carry it behind Jesus.

Julian reading
And I was filled full of compassion for all my fellow-Christians - those much, much-loved people who shall be saved. For God's servants, holy church, shall be shaken in sorrow and anguish and tribulation in this world, as a cloth is shaken in the wind...... If I look at myself alone, I am nothing. But when I think of myself and all my fellow-Christians joined together in love, I have hope. For in this joining lies the life of all who shall be saved...... And so he looks on us with love, and wants to make us his partner in good deeds.

Prayers Lord, who accepted the help of an unwilling stranger to carry your Cross, make use of us even when we have become strangers to you through sin.
All Hear us and heal us, O Lord.

Leader Let us proclaim the mystery of our redemption
All Lord, by your cross and resurrection you have set us free. You are the saviour of the world.

VI. VERONICA WIPES CHRIST'S FACE

The revelation of the glory of God in the face of Jesus

2 Cor 4: 6

Leader We adore you O Christ and we bless you
All Because by your Holy Cross you have redeemed the world.

Isaiah 53: 2-3
Without beauty, without majesty (we saw him),
no looks to attract our eyes;
a thing despised and rejected by men,
a man of sorrows and familiar with suffering,
a man to make people screen their faces;
he was despised and we took no account of him.

Julian reading
It made me think of the holy handkerchief in Rome which he has imprinted with his own blessed face when he was in great suffering, embracing death at his own will..... Many people marvel at the sadness and thinness of the likeness - when they know that he who marked it with his blessed face is the glory of heaven, flower of earth and fruit of the virgin's womb. Then how should this image be so discoloured and so far from fair? ....The meaning is this - it was the token and likeness of our dark cloak of foul black deeds that hid our beautiful, bright, blessed Lord. But I dare to say full surely, and we should believe it, that there never was so fair a man as he, until his brightness was clouded by toil and sorrow, suffering and dying.

Prayers Lord, who printed the image of your face on a white linen cloth, print your image in our hearts so we carry it always within us.
All Hear us and heal us, O Lord.

Leader Let us proclaim the mystery of our redemption
All Lord, by your cross and resurrection you have set us free.
You are the saviour of the world.

VII. CHRIST FALLS A SECOND TIME

He was despised and rejected. He was bruised for our iniquities. Isa 53: 3, 5

Leader We adore you O Christ and we bless you
All Because by your Holy Cross you have redeemed the world

Matthew 16: 24 & 25
Jesus said to his disciples, "If anyone wants to be a follower of mine, let him renounce himself and take up his cross and follow me. For anyone who wants to save his life will lose it; but anyone who loses his life for my sake will find it."

Julian reading
When Adam fell, God's son fell. For the holy joining that was made in heaven means that God's son could not be separated from Adam, and by Adam I mean all men. Adam fell from life to death in the pit of this miserable world, and after that he fell into hell….. God's son fell with Adam, into the depths of the virgin's womb - who was Adam's fairest daughter. And he did it to take away Adam's blame, both in heaven and on earth - and with great power he fetched him back from hell.

Prayers Lord, who fell beneath the weight of the Cross, open our eyes to the pain and injury our sins inflict, so we may come to hate sin as you hate it and love truth as you love it. Turn our bitterness to hope.
All Hear us and heal us, O Lord.

Leader Let us proclaim the mystery of our redemption
All Lord, by your cross and resurrection you have set us free. You are the saviour of the world.

VIII. CHRIST MEETS THE WOMEN OF JERUSALEM

Weep not for me. Weep for yourselves and for your children

Luke 23: 27-31

Leader We adore you O Christ and we bless you
All Because by your Holy Cross you have redeemed the world.

Luke 23: 27-31
Large numbers of people followed him, and of women, too, who mourned and lamented for him. But Jesus turned to them and said: "Daughters of Jerusalem, do not weep for me; weep rather for yourselves and for your children. For the days will surely come when people will say, 'Happy are those who are barren, the wombs that have never borne, the breasts that have never suckled!' Then they will begin to say to the mountains, 'Fall on us!'; to the hills, 'Cover us!' For if men use the green wood like this, what will happen when it is dry?"

Julian reading
Here our courteous Lord showed the weeping and wailing of the soul, meaning this: "I know full well that you want to live gladly and merrily because of my love, bearing all the penance that may come to you. But, since you cannot live without sin, you have to suffer - for my love - all the sorrow, all the trouble, all the unhappiness that comes upon you. And this is so. But do not be too downcast by the sin that overcomes you against your will." .... And here I understood that our Lord looks on his servant with pity, not with blame.

Prayers Lord who told the women "Weep for yourselves and for your children", comfort our grief and accept the tears we weep for you as tokens of our love and signs of our repentance.
All Hear us and heal us, O Lord.

Leader Let us proclaim the mystery of our redemption
All Lord, by your cross and resurrection you have set us free. You are the saviour of the world.

IX. CHRIST FALLS A THIRD TIME

He was despised, rejected, a man of sorrows and acquainted with grief Isa 53 :3

Leader We adore you O Christ and we bless you
All Because by your Holy Cross you have redeemed the world.

John 12: 23-26
Jesus replied to them: "Now the hour has come for the Son of man to be glorified. I tell you most solemnly, unless a wheat grain falls on the ground and dies, it remains only a single grain; but if it dies, it yields a rich harvest. Anyone who loves his life loses it; anyone who hates his life in this world will keep it for eternal life."

Julian reading
If there is a lover of God anywhere on earth who is always kept safe from falling, I know nothing of it - for it was not shown me. But this was shown - that in falling and rising again we are always held close in one love.... For our courteous Lord does not want his servants to fall into despair even when we fall into sin. For our falling does not stop him loving us.

Prayers Lord, who fell beneath the weight of the Cross, open our eyes to the pain and injury our sins inflict, so we may come to hate sin as you hate it and love truth as you love it. Turn our bitterness to hope.
All: Hear us and heal us, O Lord.

Leader Let us proclaim the mystery of our redemption
All Lord, by your cross and resurrection you have set us free. You are the saviour of the world.

X. CHRIST IS STRIPPED OF HIS CLOTHES

Being made in the likeness of humankind, he humbled himself

Phil 2: 5-11

Leader We adore you O Christ and we bless you

All Because by your Holy Cross you have redeemed the world.

John 19: 23-24
When the soldiers had finished crucifying Jesus they took his clothing and divided it into four shares, one for each soldier. His undergarment was seamless, woven in one piece from neck to hem; so they said to one another "Instead of tearing it, let us cast lots to decide who is to have it."

Julian reading
In this stark word 'sin' our Lord brought to my mind all things in general that are not good - and the shame, the despising and the utter stripping he accepted for us in this life - and his dying. He also brought to mind all the bodily and spiritual pains and passions of his creatures….. For we are all stripped in part - and shall be - while we follow our master Jesus, until we are made pure... And at this time our Lord showed me a part of his homely loving. I saw that he is everything that is good and comforting to us. He is our clothing. In his love he wraps and holds us. He enfolds us in love and he will never let us go.

Prayers Lord, who was stripped of every last possession, strip our hearts of all the things we cling to that come between our lives and your love. Lay us bare to your calling.
All Hear us and heal us, O Lord.

Leader Let us proclaim the mystery of our redemption
All Lord, by your cross and resurrection you have set us free. You are the saviour of the world.

XI . CHRIST IS NAILED TO THE CROSS

I lay down my life of my own free will. No one takes it from me.
John 10: 18

Leader We adore you O Christ and we bless you
All Because by your Holy Cross you have redeemed the world.

Luke 23: 33-34
When they reached the place called The Skull, they crucified him there and the two criminals also, one on the right, the other on the left. Jesus said, "Father forgive them; they do not know what they are doing."

Julian reading
Here I saw a great communion between Christ and ourselves, for when he was in pain, we were in pain. All creation capable of feeling pain suffered with him.... The blessed body hung alone there for a long time, and the nails wrenched it as the weight of the body pulled against it. For I understood that, because of the softness of the tender hands and feet, the huge, hard, hurtful nails pulled the wounds wide open. And the body sagged with the weight of its long hanging... And although the pain of it was sharp and bitter, it was also long drawn out.... This Showing of Christ's pain filled me full of pain, for though I knew well he suffered only once, yet it was his will to show it to me, and fill my mind with it, as I had often asked before.

Prayers Lord who let the nails be hammered home when angels could have saved you, help us to understand the wonder of your love that did not grudge the price of our redemption, but joyfully accepted suffering for our sake.
All Hear us and heal us, O Lord.

Leader Let us proclaim the mystery of our redemption
All Lord, by your cross and resurrection you have set us free. You are the saviour of the world.

XII. CHRIST DIES ON THE CROSS

And I, when I am lifted up from the earth, will draw all people to me John 12: 32

Leader We adore you O Christ and we bless you
All Because by your Holy Cross you have redeemed the world.

Luke 23: 44-46 & 49
It was now about the sixth hour and, with the sun eclipsed, a darkness came over the whole land until the ninth hour. The veil of the Temple was torn right down the middle; and when Jesus had cried out with a loud voice, he said "Father, into your hands I commend my spirit." With these words he breathed his last... All his friends stood at a distance; so also did the women who had accompanied him from Galilee, and they saw all this happen.

Julian reading
I looked for the moment of his death with all my strength and thought to have seen him quite lifeless, but I did not see him so. And just as the same moment, it seemed, that I thought that life could last no longer and the sight of his end must be shown, suddenly, as I looked on that same cross, his expression changed to joy… This change in his blessed mood changed mine, and I was as glad and merry as can be. Then our Lord brought this gladly into my mind: "Where is any part of your pain and grief now?" And I was overjoyed…And the reason why he suffers is that it is his will, in his goodness, to make us heirs with him of his joy. And, in exchange for this little pain that we suffer here, we shall have a high endless knowledge of God, which we could never have had without it.

Prayers Lord who died on the cross and rescued the souls you had been sent to save, join us fast to you in your death so we may be joined with you in your kingdom. Teach us that nothing in life or death can separate us from you.
All Hear us and heal us, O Lord.

Leader Let us proclaim the mystery of our redemption
All Lord, by your cross and resurrection you have set us free. You are the saviour of the world.

XIII. CHRIST IS TAKEN DOWN FROM THE CROSS

He that descended is the same that ascended Eph 4: 9

Leader We adore you O Christ and we bless you
All Because by your Holy Cross you have redeemed the world.

Mark 15: 42-47

It was now evening, and since it was Preparation Day (that is, the vigil of the sabbath) there came Joseph of Arimathaea, a prominent member of the Council, who himself lived in the hope of seeing the kingdom of God, and he went boldly to Pilate and asked for the body of Jesus. Pilate, astonished that he should have died so soon, summoned the centurion and enquired if he was already dead. Having been assured of this by the centurion, he granted the corpse to Joseph who brought a shroud and took Jesus down from the cross.

Julian reading

The firmament, the very earth itself, began to lose their nature with sorrow at the time of Christ's dying. For it is part of their nature to know and acknowledge him from whom their virtue springs as their God. So when his strength left him, their strength left them too, in sympathy, as far as it could, in grief at his pain. And all men in general - that is to say, even those who did not know him - had to bear the loss of every kind of comfort, except the deep, quiet keeping of God .... And so was our Lord Jesus made nothing for us, and we are all made nothing with him - and shall be nothing until we come to his bliss.

Prayers Lord, whose friends knew the death of hope when you lay lifeless in their arms, bring us hope when all seems hopeless and faith when we have lost our way, and do not forsake us, when we forsake you.
All Hear us and heal us, O Lord.

Leader Let us proclaim the mystery of our redemption
All Lord, by your cross and resurrection you have set us free. You are the saviour of the world

XIV. CHRIST IS LAID IN THE TOMB

We are buried with him in our baptism. We are raised to new life with him Rom 6: 4f

Leader We adore you O Christ and we bless you
All Because by your Holy Cross you have redeemed the world.

Matthew 27: 62-66

Next day, that is when Preparation Day was over, the chief priests and the Pharisees went in a body to Pilate and said to him: "Your Excellency, we recall that this imposter said, while he was still alive, 'After three days I shall rise again.' Therefore give orders to have the sepulchre kept secure until the third day, for fear his disciples come and steal him away and tell the people 'He has risen from the dead'." .."You may have your guard", said Pilate to them. "Go and make all as secure as you know how." So they went and made the sepulchre secure, putting seals on the stone and mounting a guard.

Julian reading

His body was in the grave until Easter morning and from that time he never lay down again. For then the moaning and groaning was rightly at an end. And our mortal flesh that God's son took upon him, which was Adam's old shirt - narrow threadbare and short - was then made beautiful by our Saviour... And so now we have matter for mourning, because our sin is the cause of Christ's pain. And we have lasting cause to rejoice, because of the endless love that made him suffer.

Prayers Lord whose home is heaven yet whose body lay in a stranger's grave, help us to know that there is no place so mean that you will not enter it, and no place so dark that you will not fill it with your light. Grant us your peace.
All Hear us and heal us, O Lord.

Leader Let us proclaim the mystery of our redemption
All Lord, by your cross and resurrection you have set us free. You are the saviour of the world.

THE JULIAN READINGS

The modern text of The Revelations of Divine Love by Julian of Norwich is from *All Shall Be Well by Sheila Upjohn* DLT 1992. Page references refer to this edition

I	Ch.35: p.59; Ch.33: p.54
II	Ch.12: p.19 & 20
III	Ch.12: 19 & 20
IV	Ch.18: p.29; Ch.7: p.7
V	Ch.28: p.46; Ch.9: p.10; Ch.43: p.82
VI	Ch.10: p.14 & 15
VII	Ch.51: p.107
VIII	Ch.82: p.185; Ch.86: p.191
IX	Ch.82: p.186; Ch.39: p.69
X	Ch.27: p.44; Ch.5: p.4
XI	Ch.18: p.29; Ch.17: p.27 & 28; Ch.16: p.26
XII	Ch.21: p.33, 34 & 35
XIII	Ch.18: p.29; Ch.52: p.113
XIV	Ch.51: p.109 & 110; Ch.52: p.112